The Exxon Valdez's Deadly Oil Spill

CODE RED
MARCH 24, 1989

by Linda Ward Beech

Consultant: Paul F. Johnston
Washington, D.C.

BEARPORT
PUBLISHING

New York, New York

Credits

Publisher: Kenn Goin
Project Editor: Adam Siegel
Creative Director: Spencer Brinker
Photo Researcher: Jennifer Bright
Design: Dawn Beard Creative

Library of Congress Cataloging-in-Publication Data

Beech, Linda.
 The Exxon Valdez's deadly oil spill / by Linda Ward Beech.
   p. cm. — (Code red)
 Includes bibliographical references and index.
 ISBN-13: 978-1-59716-366-8 (library binding)
 ISBN-10: 1-59716-366-X (library binding)
 1. Exxon Valdez Oil Spill, Alaska, 1989—Juvenile literature. 2. Oil spills—Environmental aspects—Alaska—Prince William Sound Region—Juvenile literature. 3. Tankers—Accidents—Environmental aspects—Alaska—Prince William Sound Region—Juvenile literature. 4. Exxon Valdez (Ship)—Juvenile literature. I. Title.

TD427.P4B44 2007
 363.738'2097983—dc22
                                    2006030595

For more information, write to Bearport Publishing Company, Inc., 101 Fifth Avenue, Suite 6R, New York, New York 10003. Printed in the United States of America.

10 9 8 7 6 5 4 3 2 1

Contents

Serious Trouble

It was just after midnight on Friday, March 24, 1989. The giant oil **tanker** *Exxon Valdez* was sailing through Prince William **Sound**.

Three hours earlier, the huge ship had left the **port** of Valdez, Alaska. It was carrying 53 million gallons (201 million liters) of oil to Long Beach, California.

The *Exxon Valdez* is 987 feet (301 m) long and 166 feet (50.5 m) wide. It is about as long as three football fields.

Suddenly, **Third Mate** Gregory Cousins called the captain. "I think we're in serious trouble!" said Cousins.

His words could not have been more true. While turning, the tanker had crashed into a rocky **reef**. The accident had ripped open eight huge oil tanks on board. Sticky black oil was now gushing into the sound.

The town of Valdez is at the end of the Trans-Alaska Pipeline System. The pipeline carries oil 800 miles (1,287 km) across Alaska. Tankers then pick up the oil in Valdez and bring it to other U.S. cities.

The Trans-Alaska Pipeline

A Race Against Time

Around 1:05 Friday morning, Dan Lawn's phone rang. Lawn worked for Alaska's Department of **Environmental Conservation**. For him, the news of the spill was a nightmare. Lawn knew it would be a race against time to clean up the oil. Millions of animals would soon be in danger.

Before the *Valdez* accident, Lawn had told the government that a major oil spill was likely. Unfortunately, his warnings were ignored.

Each spring, **flocks** of birds **migrate** to Prince William Sound. Bald eagles soar over the shore. Fish, sea otters, and whales swim through the chilly water. Few of them could survive such a deadly spill.

By 3:40 A.M., Lawn's speedboat had reached the tanker. "The oil was just rolling out of the bottom," he recalled.

Animals that live in Prince William Sound depend on the water for homes and food.

Unprepared

The situation grew worse every minute. Oil was flowing rapidly into the water. Lawn called the Alyeska Pipeline Service Company again and again. Its workers were supposed to respond to oil spills within about five hours. More than six hours had passed. Where were they?

A sea lion coated in oil

Sea animals could not escape the oil that spilled into the sound. They soon became coated in the sticky black liquid.

Unfortunately, Alyeska was not prepared for the spill. The cleanup equipment it needed was packed away in a warehouse. Workers had to find it and load it onto a **barge**. The barge that would carry the equipment was not ready yet, either. It was not even in the water.

> **"**I was told by Alyeska that cleanup equipment was on the way. Well, it wasn't on the way. The barge got there about 13 hours later.**"**
>
> –Dan Lawn, speaking to the *Anchorage Press*

Oil covered the waters of Prince William Sound.

Finding Help

By late Friday night, a second tanker, the *Exxon Baton Rouge*, had come to help. Unfortunately, it was too late. About 11 million gallons (42 million liters) of oil had already flooded into the sound. Who would clean up all the oil? Alyeska did not have enough equipment for the massive job.

After the accident, about 42 million gallons (159 million liters) of oil remained on board the *Valdez*. This oil was moved to the *Exxon Baton Rouge*, shown here on the right.

The *Exxon Valdez* spill was one of the largest oil spills in U.S. history.

At noon on Saturday, the Exxon company took charge. Workers tested new ways to clean up the spilled oil using chemicals and fire. Perhaps they could clean up the **polluted** water before too much wildlife was destroyed.

By Sunday, however, the cleanup had not gotten far. The weather turned stormy. Strong winds and **tides** dashed the oil onto the shore.

Oil spread along Alaska's shoreline. It oozed under the rocks and into the ground.

" The cleanup is not proceeding well. . . . We have a mess on our hands. "

—Frank Iarossi, president of Exxon Shipping

Wildlife Disaster

People who lived near the sound were worried. Would oil **contaminate** their sources of food? Concerned residents went out to the water and saw a heartbreaking sight.

Dead and dying animals were floating on the oily waves. Some had washed up on the shore. The oil had killed billions of fish and shellfish, such as clams, shrimp, and mussels.

When oil gets whipped around with sea water, it forms a gummy mixture that coats whatever it touches, such as this brown bear.

Disaster also struck seabirds, such as ducks, swans, geese, and loons. They got oil on their wings while diving for food. Their oily feathers no longer kept them warm in the icy waters. The damaged feathers also made it impossible for the birds to fly.

More than 250,000 seabirds died as a result of the oil spill. About 250 bald eagles died, too.

A seabird covered in oil

66 When I got on the beaches and got alone, I just cried like a baby.99

—Stan Stephens, a tour boat owner, after the oil spill

To the Rescue

People from around the world saw pictures of the struggling wildlife. Many wanted to help. **Volunteers** hurried to Alaska from other states. Some even came from other countries. The small town of Valdez soon became very crowded.

Recovery crews found dead sea otters coated in oil.

Many volunteers helped rescue sea otters. With oil covering their thick fur, the animals could not stay warm. Some otters tried to lick their fur clean. However, the oil made them very sick.

Heroic rescuers worked long hours. They washed the small animals with warm water and soap. They gave them medical treatment. Still, about 3,500 to 5,500 sea otters died.

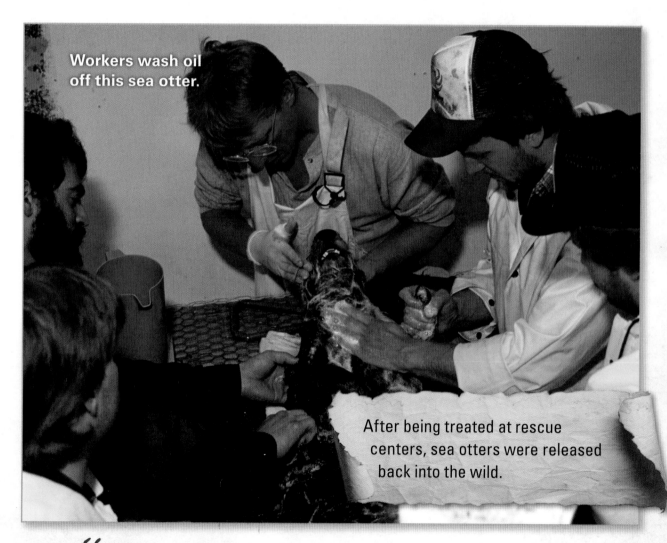

Workers wash oil off this sea otter.

After being treated at rescue centers, sea otters were released back into the wild.

“We were shocked by the number of sea otters affected by the oil.”
—Roland Smith, volunteer at the Otter Rescue Center

Cleanup

In the following weeks, more than 10,000 new workers crowded into Valdez. Exxon hired people from all over the country to help with the cleanup. Many workers lived on big barges in the water. People called these floating hotels "floatels."

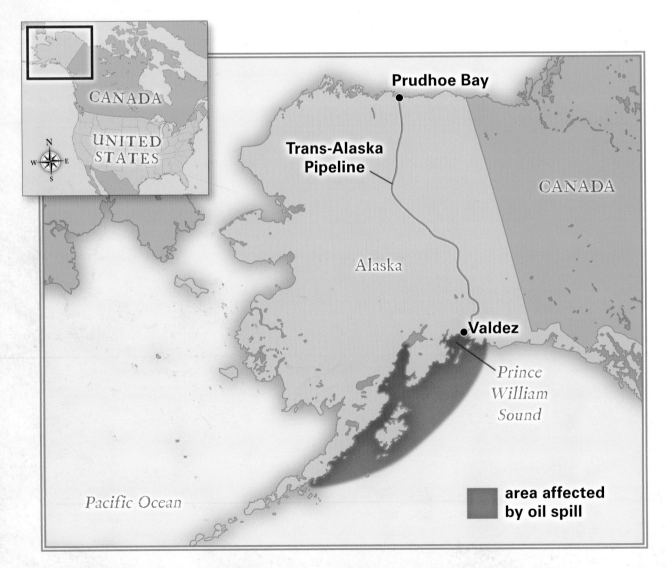

The oil that was spilled in Prince William Sound spread along 1,500 miles (2,414 km) of Alaska's coastline.

Cleaning beaches was hard work. Crews sprayed the shoreline with hot water. They also used special **bacteria** that "ate" the oil. Other workers used equipment to skim the sticky oil from the water's surface.

Cleaning a beach once wasn't always enough. The tide might change and wash more oil onto the rocks. Then the crew had to start cleaning all over again.

Workers hosed beaches with hot water to clean off the oil.

The cleanup lasted from March 1989 through June 1992. It ended more than three years after the spill. The cost was about $2.2 billion.

Rags were used to soak up the oil off rocks.

A Community of Plants and Animals

The plants and animals in Prince William Sound were all part of one **ecosystem**. They depended on the water for a place to live. They needed one another for food.

Tragically, the oil spill destroyed many of the ecosystem's **food chains**. Thousands of fish died, so seals lost their food. When seals died, killer whales lost their food, too.

When the oil spill killed crabs and other sea creatures, sea otters lost much of their food.

People were also part of this ecosystem. It was no longer safe to eat plants and animals from the sound. Like the animals, people lost part of their food supply due to the spill. They had depended on some of the wildlife from the water for food.

❝ The spill made me realize how important our food source is to us. It's everything; it's who we are.❞

–Nancy Yeaton, a community leader in the village of Nanwalek, Alaska

People fished in Prince William Sound for both food and fun. After the accident, many people lost their fishing jobs, as the fish were no longer safe to eat.

Whose Fault?

After the accident, people had many questions. Why weren't oil tankers built to be stronger? Why wasn't cleanup equipment ready? People blamed the oil companies, especially Exxon, for the disaster.

The state of Alaska and the U.S. government took the company to court. The case ended when Exxon agreed to pay about $1 billion in **settlements**.

People across the United States, such as these protesters in New Jersey, refused to buy oil from Exxon because of the spill in Alaska.

Many people also blamed Joseph Hazelwood, the ship's captain, for causing the accident. He had been drinking alcohol before boarding the tanker.

In 1990, a jury in Alaska found Hazelwood guilty of being careless. He was fined $50,000. He also had to do 1,000 hours of **community service**.

In 2006, Alaska and the U.S. government took steps to claim more money from Exxon. They asked for $92.2 million to clean up oil still in Prince William Sound.

As part of his community service, Joseph Hazelwood worked in the kitchen of a shelter for homeless people.

People Demand Change

News reports about the oil spill got people's attention. Citizens across the country demanded changes to prevent new disasters.

In 1990, the U.S. Congress passed the Oil Pollution Act (OPA). This law called for double **hulls** on all tankers by 2015. If one hull is damaged, the second one will still keep the oil from escaping. The bottom of the *Exxon Valdez* had a double hull, but its sides did not.

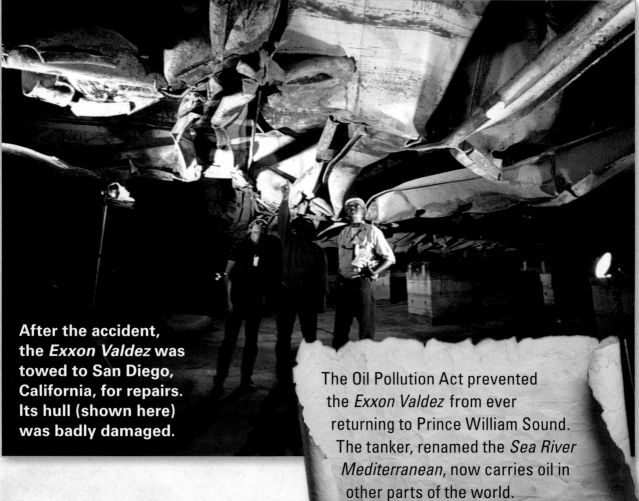

After the accident, the *Exxon Valdez* was towed to San Diego, California, for repairs. Its hull (shown here) was badly damaged.

The Oil Pollution Act prevented the *Exxon Valdez* from ever returning to Prince William Sound. The tanker, renamed the *Sea River Mediterranean*, now carries oil in other parts of the world.

A system for preventing and handling emergencies was also put in place. Today, every tanker going through Prince William Sound travels with boats that are part of the Ship Escort/Response Vessel System (SERVS). These boats help tankers move safely through the water. They also carry equipment for dealing with oil spills.

This tug boat (right) is part of the Ship Escort/Response Vessel System. It travels with tankers to help prevent oil spills in Prince William Sound.

Learning from the Mess

Slowly, some parts of Prince William Sound began returning to normal. After seven years, Herring Bay showed no signs of oil. Beaches in other areas, like Smith Island, stayed oily 17 years later.

In 1990, scientists began studies in 20 different places. They wanted to see how the sound had recovered.

Every year, researchers visit the locations of their studies. They check each place for oil and count the plants and animals living there.

Nearly 14,000 oil spills are reported each year in the United States alone.

The scientists learned some surprising things. For example, some adult animals such as clams may live on oily beaches. However, their young cannot.

Scientists also realized that hosing beaches caused terrible damage. The blasts of hot water had washed away many plants. Some never grew back. Researchers hope this information will help people better handle future oil spills.

Sometimes scientists had to dig deep underneath the surface to check if oil was still left on the beaches.

“It's not something that people can easily forget. To some extent, the resources are recovering. But the people still hurt.”
—Gary Kompkoff, fisherman

Today and Tomorrow

After the cleanup, many people continued working to restore Prince William Sound. Groups like the Prince William Soundkeeper help keep the beaches clean and reduce pollution.

People did not quickly forget the *Exxon Valdez* oil spill. In 1999, this woman displayed oil-covered stones from Prince William Sound to remind people of the disaster that took place ten years earlier.

In May 1998, the state started the Alaska SeaLife Center in Seward. It also bought 650,000 acres (263,046 hectares) of forest and coastal land to protect the animals there.

Prince William Sound is once again a place of great beauty. In many ways, it is healthy again. People living there are doing all they can to keep it that way.

Communities started new projects using money from the fines Exxon paid. In one program, students took photos to keep track of killer whales.

Profiles

Many people played an important role in the events connected to the *Exxon Valdez* oil spill. Here are four of them.

Frank Iarossi was the president of Exxon Shipping at the time of the *Valdez* accident.

- Shared information about the accident with the public
- Spoke to the press and angry crowds every day following the spill
- Resigned from Exxon in 1990
- Later become the leader of a company that makes sure ships are safe enough to go to sea

Riki Ott is a scientist and an expert on oil pollution.

- Spoke about oil spills to the mayor of Valdez and others the night before the accident
- Worked with the fishing community and was a fisher herself
- Wrote a book about the spill
- Still works to protect the environment

Dan Lawn worked for Alaska's Department of Environmental Conservation.

- Helped design the oil terminal at Valdez
- Worked as an inspector of oil tankers for the state of Alaska
- Spent ten years recording problems with oil companies
- Had warned the state about oil disasters in Prince William Sound

Terrie Williams is a scientist from California.

- Researched sea otters for many years
- Traveled to Prince William Sound to help after the oil spill
- Set up an emergency hospital for oily sea otters

Glossary

bacteria (bak-TIHR-ee-uh) tiny life forms that can be seen only under a microscope

barge (BARJ) a flat-bottomed boat that is used to carry things

community service (kuh-MYOO-nuh-tee SUR-viss) work for a good cause that a person chooses or is ordered by a court to do without pay

contaminate (kuhn-TAM-uh-nayt) to make something dirty, polluted, or unfit for use

ecosystem (EE-koh-*siss*-tuhm) all the animals and plants that live together in a certain environment

environmental conservation (en-*vye*-ruhn-MENT-uhl *kon*-sur-VAY-shuhn) the protection of plants, animals, and other natural resources

flocks (FLOKS) groups of birds or other animals that live and travel together

food chains (FOOD CHAYNZ) series of plants and animals that depend on one another for food

hulls (HUHLZ) the outer skins (sides and bottoms) of tankers or other ships

migrate (MYE-grate) to move from one place to another at a certain time of the year

polluted (puh-LOOT-id) dirty, due to harmful material, such as smoke or waste, being added to air, soil, or water

port (PORT) a place where ships load and unload cargo

reef (REEF) a ridge of rock, sand, or coral that lies near the surface of a body of water

settlements (SET-uhl-muhnts) legal agreements

sound (SOUND) a body of water connected to the ocean that usually runs along the coast

tanker (TANG-kur) a ship that carries liquids, such as oil

third mate (THURD MATE) an officer on a ship who ranks below the captain, first mate, and second mate

tides (TIDEZ) the movement of water toward or away from the shore of an ocean or any large body of water

volunteers (*vol*-uhn-TIHRZ) people who work by choice without pay

Bibliography

Leacock, Elspeth. *The* Exxon Valdez *Oil Spill*. New York: Facts on File (2005).

Walker, Jane. *Oil Spills*. Mankato, MN: Stargazer Books (2004).

Exxon Valdez Oil Spill Trustee Council (**www.evostc.state.ak.us/**)

National Oceanic & Atmospheric Administration (**www.noaa.gov/**)

Prince William Sound Regional Citizens' Advisory Council (**www.pwsrcac.org/**)

Read More

Berger, Melvin. *Oil Spill!* New York: HarperCollins (1994).

Harris, Joan. *One Wing's Gift: Rescuing Alaska's Wild Birds*. Portland, OR: Alaska Northwest Books (2002).

Sherrow, Victoria. *The* Exxon Valdez*: Tragic Oil Spill*. Berkeley Heights, NJ: Enslow Publishers (1998).

Smith, Roland. *Sea Otter Rescue: The Aftermath of an Oil Spill*. New York: Puffin Books (1999).

Learn More Online

To learn more about the *Exxon Valdez* oil spill, visit **www.bearportpublishing.com/CodeRed**

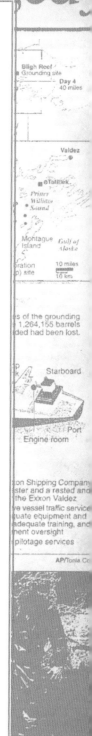

Index

About the Author

Linda Ward Beech has written more than 60 books for students and teachers. She has also taught reading to adults and has worked as a volunteer teacher at P.S. 199 in New York City. Her hobbies are bicycling, gardening, baking, and reading.